CW00829464

TRANSLATION IN PRACTICE

Library of Congress Cataloging-in-Publication Data

Translation in practice : a symposium / edited by Gill Paul. -- 1st ed.
    p. cm.
  Includes bibliographical references.
  ISBN 978-1-56478-548-0 (pbk. : acid-free paper)
  1. Translating and interpreting--Congresses. I. Paul, Gill.
P306T738 2009
418'.02--dc22

                                   2009001347

Partially funded by grants from Arts Council England and the Illinois Arts
Council, a state agency; and supported by the British Centre for Literary
Translation, The Society of Authors, the British Council, and by the Univer-
sity of Illinois at Urbana-Champaign.

www.dalkeyarchive.com

Cover: design by Danielle Dutton, illustration by Nicholas Motte
Printed on permanent/durable acid-free paper and bound in the
United States of America

TRANSLATION IN PRACTICE

a symposium
edited by Gill Paul

Dalkey Archive Press ▣ Champaign and London

CONTENTS

CHAPTER FIVE: THE EDITING PROCESS

CHAPTER SIX: ONGOING RELATIONSHIPS

PREFACE
by Amanda Hopkinson
Director, British Centre for Literary Translation

The need is clear. The most frequently asked questions fielded by the British Centre for Literary Translation relate to such issues as, 'What is the role of my editor?', 'Will he or she know the language(s) I translate from?', 'Should I discuss the translation with the original author?' and 'Who has the last word on what stands?'

Questions were both asked and addressed—at length—during a one-day discussion on the topic of editing held in March 2008 at the British Council offices in London. Funded by Arts Council, London, administrated by The Society of Authors, devised by literary translator Ros Schwartz, and inspired by a handbook produced by the Norwegian Translators' Association, the forum and this publication, from which it derives, are the fruit of the collective effort of the above parties. Intended to accommodate 50 participants, admission had to be stretched to admit over 90. To round off the day of discussion and debate, the group split into workshops that busily learned how to translate through practice—with no prior knowledge of the language required!

Essentially this is a very practical handbook. Practically, it may well become an essential one. As well as answering a number of obvious—and a few recondite—queries, it provides welcome doses of optimism and encouragement. Yes, editors and even authors have been known to work happily with their translators. A very few writ-

i

ers even want to share credits and profits more generously than the terms stipulated by the Translators' Association model contract (a basic working tool of any literary translator worth their salt). Portuguese Nobel Prizewinner Jose Saramago is one such example, who kindly insists: 'Lamentably, I can only write books in Portuguese. It is my translators on whom I rely to render my books universal.'

Saramago may be a delight for a translator to work with; other authors may not, or they may be long since departed. Enter the editor, a translator's 'first reader,' bar the customary recourse to spouses and pets. In order not to feel neglected or competed with, a translator needs to feel that her approach—if possible, even some elementary problems—are understood and can be addressed. The narrative voice or voices are all: achieving their best possible expression is the over-riding task of editor and translator working together.

Thus far, this preface has been composed from the standpoint with which my work has made me most familiar. Read on and this handbook adopts a 360-degree approach, involving both publishers and the editors themselves. Already, it is set to become a staple for publishing courses and diplomas in tertiary education, for professional associations (such as The Society for Editors and Proofreaders), for workshops run by any of these, and for the many individuals employed across the field of literary translation.

In short, anyone who wishes to know more about the path from foreign original to target translation, and who further wishes for it to be as straight as possible, will find this handbook is a vital and stimulating requirement.

INTRODUCTION: THE AIM OF A GOOD TRANSLATION

Readers of literary fiction have high expectations. They demand a book be rich, dense and multidimensional, capable of weaving magic and changing something, no matter how small, about the way they perceive themselves. They also want to be entertained, but on an intelligent level. An author who can create such fiction must have insight, a mastery of language, a compelling sense of rhythm, idiom and nuance, and the ability to transform inspiration into a stunning and transcendent work of art.

When literary works are translated, the translator's job is to *recreate* this work of art sensitively and seamlessly in such a way that it is true to the original, as well as being equally enchanting, poetic and perceptive. Grace, beauty, colour and flavour must be captured, and the resulting work must also be capable of being understood by its new audience, and make sense on every level. A translation should have the same virtues as the original, and inspire the same response in its readers. It must reflect cultural differences, while drawing parallels that make it accessible, and it must achieve a fine balance between the literal and the suggestive, the story and its melody. It should be read by readers in its new language with the same enthusiasm and understanding as it was in the old.

And so the role of a translator is many-faceted. He or she must hear the music of the original, and replay it for a new audience; a good translation sings, and displays a rhythm that not only reflects the original text's origin but also beats to a new drum. A translator is both reader and writer; a translation is undoubtedly one person's subjective reading of the source text, and, inevitably, it is reflected through that translator's subjectivity. No two translators, like no two readers, are the same. Words have different resonances and connotations for everyone, and when a translator works, he or she dredges up expressions, interpretations, vocabulary and insight from a host of subconscious pools of language and experience.

In the words of one translator, 'Literary translation involves making endless choices, weighing up whether to privilege meaning over music, rhythm over rules of grammar, spirit rather than letter of text, in order to give a translation its distinctive voice, while conveying the many layers of the original in a way that preserves the author's intentions.'

Incumbent to this process, and often the enthusiastic originator of the project, is the acquiring editor at the publishing house, who has felt the vibrations and spirit of the original, and has invested time and energy in ensuring that it will be recreated in equal measure in English. Negotiating a balance between producing a commercially viable book and one that stays true to the author's vision and literary genius is never easy. The process through which a foreign language text is translated into English can represent a minefield of potential dangers, all of which could hamper the eventual success of the book, and even affect the viability of continuing to publish future titles in translation. And yet, success is not only possible but also achievable, by taking steps to ensure that best practice is employed at every stage.

Increased globalisation and widespread immigration have made readers more aware of cultural anomalies and more open to fresh ideas, different insights, and alternative observations. Many of the titles on the UK bestseller lists are set in countries that have hugely diverse cultures and concerns. There is a refreshing surge in interest in the unusual and even the obscure; perhaps a better way of putting it is that modern-day readers are content to explore differences.

And so a whole new world has opened up, and the process of feeding this demand, and doing justice to an industry that is not only growing but, in some cases, bursting at its seams, requires a stealthy and well-considered hand. Translators are an essential link in the creative process; editors are the seers and the go-betweens, the filter through which translated material becomes the published article.

It is, therefore, hugely important that both translator and editor establish the best way to operate, to keep one another happy and motivated, to form a healthy and successful relationship that will not only benefit the book in question, but also the success of translations in general, to ensure that every stage of the translation and editing process protects the quality and integrity of the original, while simultaneously creating something noteworthy to inspire fresh interest, and claim a new following. Both parties have to negotiate different courses, and both parties need to find their common ground.

And that is what this guide is about—finding and establishing best practice for both translators and editors, in order to achieve the holy grail of translation success, and create a market for increasingly diverse and interesting works by a wide variety of authors. Many editors and translators have decades of experience behind them; however, in an increasingly vibrant or even resurgent market, practice should be re-examined regularly, to establish what both editors and translators require to create the best possible finished product. Times have changed, and what may in the past have been perceived to be good practice may now be outdated, not least due to changes in communications and print technology. Similarly, the robust nature of the market means that expectations have been lifted, and translations are no longer being seen as inferior cousins to English literary fiction; in fact, they have created a market of their own. So new practices are in order, based on an understanding of the roles and responsibilities of the protagonists: author, translator, editor and publisher.

The translation of literary fiction demands much more than knowledge of two or more languages. An ability to convert words literally from one language to another is the most basic skill required by any translator; but those who translate literary fiction require something beyond this—something much more creative, involving an instinctive understanding of the way that words and phrases can work together to best effect, in order to reveal both the story and the subtle nuances that create its context and apparent intent.

As Palestinian poet and journalist Mahmoud Darwish puts it in the preface to *Poésie: La terre nous est étroite*: 'The translator is not a ferryman for the meaning of the words but the author of their web of new relations. And he is not the painter of the light part of the meaning, but the watcher of the shadow, and what it suggests.'

Good translators, particularly in languages that are popular with readers at any given time, are highly sought after. In many cases, the same translators are used on consecutive projects, and given first refusal of new translations. Most acquiring editors have their favourite top three or four translators in the principal European languages with which they normally work. They do, however, take on new translators on the strength of readers' reports and sample translations, and those with the appropriate skills should find that they are able to get work.

Many editors are happy to receive CVs from prospective translators, and normally keep these on file. Most request that any CV is accompanied by a sample translation of a literary work, of at least two to three thousand words. Many editors do not have first-hand knowledge of all of the languages they publish, so it helps them if they know the work in question. It can also help to bring yourself to an editor's notice if you take a book to them with a view to translating it for their list.

Before offering a new, untried translator a whole book to work on, editors may try them out by asking for a report on a book that's been offered to them. This is a good way of assessing whether their tastes converge.

Outside readers

Acquiring editors will commission an outside reader (often a translator) to report on a foreign-language book when it is in a language they do not read well enough themselves or if they simply don't have the time to get through all the submissions on their desk. The outside reader should be fluent in both the native language of the book and in English, and they should be conversant with the qualities the publisher is looking for in its fiction list.

The outside reader will write a report providing a summary of the book's plot, and commenting on its literary merit and making a personal recommendation about whether or not it should be published in English. The report should mention any issues of style, vocabulary and structure that might make the book difficult to translate, and also identify in advance any areas where there might be potential problems (translating humour, for example, or explaining cultural practices).

Providing an initial report need not be the end of the outside reader's role, though. He or she may be asked to comment on sample translations and be involved in the final choice of translator; to offer a link between author and English publisher, providing information on the nature of the translation and reassuring the author that various stylistic and other features integral to the book have been retained; and to judge the final merits of the translation—not from the viewpoint of a potential reader, but as an assessor of the translation's success in recreating the original.

Most outside readers are involved at several stages and when an editor is unfamiliar with the original language, they are not a luxury and should be budgeted for, and time allowed for their involvement. Some publishers like to use more than one reader to get a good overall view of the finished product.

FINDING THE RIGHT TRANSLATOR

When an editor acquires a foreign-language novel, and is excited by this 'new find,' he or she hopes to commission a translator who shares that enthusiasm.

The editor will be looking for a translator who can not only match the style of the original book, but also see beneath the words to make sense of the ideas. Even the best translator may not be appropriate for every book that comes along. Some books simply don't strike the necessary chord, or offer the right inspiration. One translator described working on several books for a publisher, and being disappointed to realise that she simply felt no affinity with a new book on offer. She didn't think that she could get into the book in a significant enough way to make it work on all levels, and declined the job.

Other obvious requirements are a deep understanding of the culture from which the book derives and in which it is set, as well as the appropriate level of intellect to translate ideas, thoughts and theories, along with the words. Books with humour require a translator with wit, and where there is an unusual or intricate use of language (in the case of dialects, slang terms, and even cadence), a good understanding of and ability to translate the spoken word is essential. If it is a book written for teenagers, incorporating teenage slang, the editor will look for a translator who has contact and sympathy with that age group. A decision may be made that a female translator is better for a book with particularly feminine subject matter, or a male for one on a particularly masculine topic. Some books focus on specialist areas, perhaps involving historical facts or scientific theory, for example. In this case, the translator should have a good working knowledge of the subject matter, or a proven ability to research, disseminate and extrapolate information successfully.

On top of all these requirements, an editor will look for a translator with whom he or she has a good rapport. Establishing good communication from the outset will make the whole translation process much smoother and more successful.

When an editor is scouting around to find the best person for a new novel, he or she might decide to commission sample translations from a few possible contenders. Even seasoned, experienced translators can be asked to provide a sample chapter in order to ensure that they have understood the essence of the book in question and can do it justice. Editors should make it very clear to all concerned if they are asking for a number of samples, and be prepared to pay the going rate for each sample translation requested (which will usually be about two or three thousand words in length). Translators should resist any publishers who expect samples to be provided free of charge. Although seemingly a quick task, samples can be time-consuming because they entail becoming familiar with the style and story of the whole book.

Ideally, editors will make clear what they are expecting from a sample translation; they may have their own ideas about how the language should work, or what features of the author's style should shine through. It is helpful if the editor provides prospective translators with as much background information about the book as possible, including any press cuttings, or interviews with the author.

From an editorial point of view, it makes sense to ask translators to work on the same sample, so that differences in approach and use of language are obvious. It has been reported that some unscrupulous publishers have lined up a series of translators to provide free or cheap samples, each for a different chapter of the book—thereby getting a translation done quickly and inexpensively. The world of translators can be very small, and many will be aware of which other translators are involved in a 'beauty contest.' In best practice, translators should always know how many other candidates are involved, and whether they are all working on the same sample of text.

Editors who have little understanding of the language being translated may use an outside reader to help make the appropriate decision, but if an English translation 'sings,' and seems to get across the style, tone and message of the original author, based on what the editor has heard about the book, this can be enough. Good translations are creative works in their own right that have the ability to do both the book and the author justice.

When the editor selects the translator he or she wants to use, it is a good idea for the translator to ask that their sample be edited. This will give an early indication of what the editor is looking for and can help to iron out some of the problems from the start (see page 38).

The author's input

It is good practice for editors to involve the author as much as possible in decisions about the book to reduce the potential for conflict further down the line. The author should be informed about the choice of translator, and shown the sample translation done by the successful candidate.

Some authors will have only a rudimentary understanding of English and will be unable to comment upon a translation in any significant way. Other authors may feel that their English is good enough for them to make an assessment of the various samples provided; but editors beware! If an author disagrees with your choice of translator on the basis of his or her understanding of English, it's worth explaining your decision. Subtle nuances and a play of words may be lost on poor English speakers, and it may be that their inability to 'understand' the translation is because it is understated and has been approached creatively to give a flavour that may only be recognised by someone familiar with English.

If an author expresses an interest in translating his or her own work, or having a friend or family member do so, it is a good idea to ask them to submit sample material, as you would any aspiring translator. Creativity and skill in one language does not necessarily mean the same in another, and familiarity with a book does not necessarily make a good translation. A beautiful book may become wooden and littered with anomalies in the hands of a poor translator, no matter what his or her provenance.

Once a translator has been chosen, he or she should be introduced to the author (by e-mail, phone or in person) and a channel of communication established. Editors can make use of the translator's verbal skills to communicate successfully with the author about the book's progress. Try to ensure that the author feels comfortable answering the translator's queries, and explaining parts of the book or a use of language that might not be entirely clear.

It is also a good idea to talk the author through any changes that you feel the book might need in order to make it understandable by and appropriate for the English language market. In some translations, whole swathes of material have to be changed or even cut in an attempt to tighten a woolly plot or lose superfluous material. A successful book is not always a perfect book, and the original editing may not have been as good as it could have been. In this case, a translation can improve the book, which will, of course, encourage its success in a market with which the author may not be familiar.

It is, of course, a huge advantage if the author has been translated before, and already has a good working relationship with a translator. If the first book was a success, and was well received in English, there is usually no reason why the same path cannot be followed again.

Using two translators

Some books call out for a combined effort. For example, a book that relies heavily on dialogue native to a particular part of a country or city may not be easily understood or converted into English by even the best translator. Similarly, specialist subjects within novels may also require two hands—one to explain the subject succinctly, another to make it readable. A good literal translation may, equally, require the secondary attentions of a more literary translator who can make it more fluent and capture the poetry of the original in a way that is appropriate for its new market.

Martin Riker, associate director at Dalkey Archive Press, a US publisher committed to publishing international works and 'giving them a home,' says the Press has used two translators on a number of titles. For example, Jon Fosse's book *Melancholy* was translated by a Norwegian native-speaker, Grethe Kvernes, working closely with prose stylist Damion Searls, who at the outset of the project had a limited knowledge of Norwegian. Together they created an extraordinarily good translation, which worked on every level. Martin explains:

'The success of such partnerships lies in the fact that writers, if they are good writers, can bring to the translation the subtlety and energy of a literary stylist. They understand that if the book is to be responsible to the original, it has to be creatively inspired like the original. One of the obstacles facing English-language translations today is that so few of our best creative writers are also translators. This does not seem to be the case in other countries where literary translations are read more widely. Fortunately, we do have plenty of excellent translators with the stylistic facility of a novelist—which is, in fact, a large part what makes those translators excellent.'

The process of translation can be a lonely and often frustrating job, and even the best translators can struggle to find exactly the right words, or to get across an idea or a theme. Many translators speak of labouring over a single word for hours or even days, or feeling dissatisfaction with particular passages for which they don't believe they've captured the author's intentions. For this reason, many translators actively enjoy the process of working in tandem. It can lengthen the process, and it can also mean a significantly reduced fee, but in many cases it works.

Ros Schwartz and Lulu Norman met through the Translators' Association and have been working together for almost ten years. They both have a strong interest in Francophone writers, and have co-translated *The Star of Algiers* by Aziz Chouaki and *The Belly of the Atlantic* by Fatou Diome.

Ros was offered the translation of *The Star of Algiers* when Lulu was too busy to take it on, and immediately fell in love with the book. She did, however, feel the style and language presented some real challenges, and suggested that they work together—she'd do the first translation, and Lulu would come in at the editing stage. Ros explains how this worked:

'The translation did indeed prove tough. Most of the time I felt as though I was wading through treacle with very heavy boots on. I worked quite fast on the first draft, leaving in different options when I was uncertain and highlighting problematic passages, of which there were many. By the end of the second draft, quite a few of these had resolved themselves, but I still had a lot of doubts and the translation hadn't gelled. I wanted to fine-tune the translation until it was as good as it possibly could be before handing it over to Lulu.

'Lulu went through the translation annotating the printout. We'd agreed that she'd jot down any thoughts and suggestions for me to incorporate as I saw fit, and then we'd meet as often as necessary to polish the final version. The manuscript came back covered in pencilled comments. Lulu was much tougher than any editor. But she was always spot on, and I accepted about 99 percent of her suggestions. It was an exhilarating feeling. Her interventions showed that the book "inhabited" her as it did me. Chouaki is a writer for whom rhythm is tremendously important—he's a jazz musician. Lulu's input was mostly to do with getting the right heartbeat for the English text. She brought a whole new vocabulary and boldness to the translation and resolved some of the passages that had me stumped.

'The last stage involved a number of caffeine-fuelled sessions sprawled on Lulu's sofa or on mine, surrounded by dictionaries and thesauruses, going over the translation line by line, reading it aloud and pausing every time something bothered one of us.

'Although we come from quite different backgrounds, we have a shared language sensibility. This is important if you are collaborating, because ultimately word choices are subjective. Lulu and I "hear" in the same way, both the author's voice and our own. When one of us said "Stop, that doesn't work," the other would invariably agree. We'd brainstorm and would both immediately recognise the "right" solution when one of us alighted on it. I don't think this is something that can be taken for granted. Collaborating on a translation requires a shared empathy for the source text and a similar feel for the "voice" and texture of the translation.'

The second book, *The Belly of the Atlantic* by Fatou Diome, a Senegalese writer living in France, was approached differently. Ros and Lulu split the book down the middle, each translating half, then annotating each other's work and coming together to thrash out the final version. Lulu says:

'I had a (possibly romantic) notion that the writer's voice might be skewed somehow by dividing the book this way and worried about evenness of tone. But by then our confidence and trust in each other had grown and our roles became both more blurred and more unified as we went over and over it, back and forth, so I didn't really know who did what. Nor did it matter.

'We all have our blind spots; everyone is constrained by their personal idiolect, by the limits of their vocabulary, by their habits, taste or prejudice—by their experience *tout court*. This is not necessarily challenged much in the course of a translation when you work alone (unless you have a very active editor—which seems less and less likely these days, if you have one at all) nor do you often have to account for it. It's simply the way you are, part of your working method and what you make use of in the translation; you take it for granted.

'And it's precisely what you take for granted that's opened up in a good collaborative process (resulting, too, in a gentle probing of your own method) and the effect is to make the book at least three times better than it would have been. When you have to externalise your thought processes, articulate and justify them, you can't help but make the work clearer. Ros and I are complementary in ways I couldn't have anticipated, and our differences make the work stronger.

'The other important factor is time, which tends to be in short supply. We're all familiar with *l'esprit d'escalier*, with second thoughts, and the involuntary nature of memory. You need, too, a period of time to turn away from the text and let your eyes become accustomed to another light before returning. In theory at least, with two translators, that interim period isn't necessary, because the work comes back altered by the other's gaze as well as their pen.

'It's unlikely, after all, that you'll both fall down at the same time or in the same place; things that seem impossible to you may be no problem to your other half. The lost feelings that can occur during a long translation are much diminished, the heavy weight of responsibility halved. There will be fewer things overlooked or which you may not have fully understood but somehow hoped would pass muster, and there's less danger of falling into some kind of private language. You also have two times the experience to bring to bear, which must enrich the work in ways you can't measure.'

In Lulu's and Ros's eyes, their collaborative efforts are the key to producing a successful book on a multitude of levels. Lulu says, 'All translators know the importance of "fresh eyes" on the translation, and I've often handed over my work to trusted colleagues to find it benefited hugely from their input.'

Many translators find it useful to share ideas, to brainstorm and negotiate different passages with the help of others. Robert Chandler, who translated *The Railway* by Hamid Ismailov, says:

'I twice read the entire translation out loud to my wife, and there are many sentences we must have discussed twenty or more times. She drew my attention to passages that were unclear, and helped me formulate questions to put to Hamid; she also contributed many phrases and some elegant puns herself, as well as making a crucial suggestion about the order of chapters.'

It is worth considering a joint effort, or encouraging a translator to collaborate, if there are areas in which they feel that working together would enhance the final product. Even in a climate of tight budgets, paying a little more for twice the number of eyes, ears and pencils can reap rewards by creating something that is as near to perfect in English as it is possible to be.

CHAPTER TWO: TRANSLATION CONTRACTS

The contract between translator and publisher is as important as that between publisher and author. In essence, the translator becomes the 'English' author of the book, and should be fairly represented and acknowledged in that role. Most translators labour over their work every bit as much as most authors do; theirs is a creative effort, and it calls upon resources that even the most successful authors may not have—in particular, an ability to recreate someone else's work of art with fluidity and sensitivity. While a translator doesn't have to come up with a plot or a series of characters, he or she will have to find every one of the 'right' words with which to convey the book's message and recreate its magic.

Translators should expect to retain copyright of their translation, and to assert their moral rights. Like an author, they will be contractually obliged to submit material of publishable quality, and according to the details agreed in advance. All contracts should, therefore, contain within them, or added as a schedule, an editorial brief that outlines the expectations of the publisher.

After an initial read-through, a translator should know which parts of the book may present difficulties, and should discuss with the editor the best ways of surmounting them: the style of language; any structural changes that might be required (not all books are translated directly from published sources; some may arrive in manuscript form, in which case the translator will also be acting as the first editor of the work); any special demands, for example, clarifying and explaining cultural or specialist features that are critical to an understanding of the book; and any liberties that will be allowed. How much poetic licence can be taken by the translator? All these issues might form part of the contractual editorial brief. We'll look at these matters in more detail in Chapter Three.

APPROVAL OF THE TEXT

In most cases, contracts state that 'reasonable changes' may be made to the translator's text by the editor, and they should add that translators have the right to approve any changes. It is difficult to phrase the contractual wording of this in a way that satisfies both translator and publisher and the term 'reasonable' can have a range of meanings.

If translators are given a clear brief at the outset and a house style sheet, this should overcome the need for niggling changes (like changing 'ise' to 'ize' endings). Editing should be about improvement, and translators must be open to the idea that their work will benefit positively from another pair of eyes. Most translators admit to becoming too close to a work to see its flaws, and it is the job of an editor to point them out and work on a solution.

'Reasonable' changes are those that the editor considers necessary to produce the best possible book. Equally, translators must be 'reasonable' in accepting that some change is necessary. Rebecca Carter, an editor at Chatto & Windus, is accustomed to making significant changes to even the best translations, and considers this an integral part of her job. She says:

'Just as writers writing in their native language need a second eye on their work, so translators can benefit from the distance another reader brings. I wouldn't consider it too much editing if I needed to make, on average, small amendments to every other sentence. That might seem quite a lot, and some translators might not need that level of editing if they have been through a rigorous editorial process with someone else (as Robert Chandler did with his wife on *The Railway*), but I don't think that fairly heavy editing implies that the translation is bad. It is simply a question of pushing against any weak spots in vocabulary or sentence structure to make sure that everything is working together as well as it should be. Translators are often delighted with my line edit, because I perhaps pick out exactly the sentences that they have tortured themselves about and suggest possible solutions that have eluded them, or suggest something that provokes in him/her the discovery of a "third way." Ideally, we'll see completely eye-to-eye and a strong relationship of trust is formed whereby the translator is happy for me to play around with the text, knowing that I will always consult him or her about any change I make, and am prepared to back down if the translator thinks I'm wrong about something.'

It would be good practice for translators to ensure that within their contracts there is a clause stating that changes must be agreed before the book is published. Translators should be given approval of the final text before it goes for setting, to ensure that mistakes or misinterpretations can be corrected before they become expensive. In many cases, this will save a lot of trouble at a later date. If editor and translator cannot resolve a difference of opinion regarding a change, it is customary for the editor to have the final say (see page 66).

All of this should be outlined in the contract, and it is the transla-tor's responsibility to ensure that his or her rights are clear at the outset.

CREDITING THE TRANSLATOR

In some cases, publishers put the translator's name on the cover of the book (in a size that is slightly smaller than that of the author). In others, usually for commercial reasons, this practice is avoided. Many marketing and sales departments believe that it can be dif-ficult to persuade readers in an English market that translations are worthwhile investments of their time and money. They don't want to draw attention to the fact that it is a translation, hoping, perhaps, to catch them unawares. Just as some cinema-goers will baulk at a subtitled film, some readers have a negative prejudice against translations, believing them to be stilted or substandard versions of the original. Some simply consider them 'hard work.' Of course, this is rarely the case, but it is necessary for translators to be realistic and to ensure that sales are maximised by approach-ing the book in a way that the publisher (in this case, the expert) believes best.

Whether or not the translator's name appears on the cover, it should always be printed on the title page, an appropriate copy-right line for the translation should appear on the title verso, and acknowledgements and dedications suggested by the translator should be included. The role of the translator should be evident to every reader who cares to look for it.

According to the 1976 UNESCO Nairobi Recommendation Concerning the International Exchange of Cultural Property, translators are considered to be authors and should be treated as such, which means they have a right to royalties on copies of the book sold. The fee offered to the translator may be an advance against these royalties. The fee or advance should be sufficient recompense for the amount of time required to complete the translation. A small fee is unacceptable if a translator is expected to spend six months or more working exclusively on the book in question.

Some translators may agree to work on a fee-only basis, the level of which can be mutually agreed. This is an individual decision.

Contracts should contain full details of the fee payment stages, the royalties and the split between author and translator for the subsequent sale of rights and for any serialization. In most cases, 80 percent of the gross proceeds go to the author, and 20 percent to the translator, or there may be a 75/25 split. This is, of course, a matter for negotiation.

If a translator is required to research extensively, perhaps including travel, a separate expenses budget may be agreed upon. Expenses should be settled on production of receipts, and should not form part of the advance against royalties.

When a book is sold in another country, even in the same language, the publisher, author and translator should benefit financially. It is usual for the publisher to take 20 percent of the gross proceeds, and split the remainder between author and translator at an agreed ratio.

The US publisher may require changes to the translation, and the same contractual terms concerning changes normally apply as for the UK edition. Unfortunately, because they are one step removed from the new publisher, who will usually deal directly with the UK editor or even just the UK rights department, translators are not always given the chance to see changes before the book is published. A contract must, therefore, be in place before the book is edited for the American market, which provides for the translator to be consulted about all changes, and states that only 'reasonable' changes may be made.

In the case of a dispute, it can occasionally be helpful to go back to the original foreign language publisher but, in reality, a non-English publisher is unlikely to be able to make clear or helpful judgements about what comprises good English.

When translators disagree with changes made to their text in any edition and no compromise can be reached, they can ask to have their names taken off the book, but this should be a last resort. Most editors will defend their translators against unfair or unnecessary changes that affect the book significantly.

There is a lively and ongoing debate between editors and translators about the question of Americanization. Translators are often disgruntled to find that foreign words that they had carefully retained to give the book the right flavour are removed in favour of their American alternatives, even when there isn't really an obvious or acceptable alternative. For example, 'flats' become 'apartments,' which may be something different altogether, and quintessential cups of tea become mugs of Starbucks.

Most translators feel strongly that it is the foreignness of a translation that sets it apart from its literary equals, and gives it its unique ambience. Ros Schwartz summarises the position clearly:

'We all, translators and editors, seem to be much more worried about "foreign" words in a translation than in a book originally written in English, but from a different culture. A very simple example: take food. I remember reading American books as a teenager where kids were always eating Hershey bars. I had no idea what a Hershey bar was, but it didn't bother me, I realised from the context that it must have been something like a Mars bar. But in a translation, we translators and our editors get anxious about French people eating a *boeuf bourguignon* or a *croque monsieur*. The foreignization/domestication debate is an important ethical question and it helps for the translator to have a clear approach and to articulate this to the publisher.

'The translator walks a tightrope between author, editor, publisher and reader. Where should our primary loyalty lie? Sometimes, if you're loyal to the author, the editor feels the text is inaccessible to the reader. But if you adapt to the limitations of the putative reader, you may feel you are being disloyal to the author. The publisher is mindful of commercial considerations and wants to ensure the book will sell, which may affect their editorial stance. It is in this tension that the translation dilemma resides, and there is no simple answer. Articulating this tension and discussing it in these terms is a step towards resolving the ethical question it raises.'

It would be helpful for translators to know in advance what the target market might be, and what that market would expect. If the translator, in trying to retain the essence of the book by including foreign terms instead of dumbing it down with inappropriate substitutions, falls foul of a particular publisher's house style or approach, it may take much more than a rewrite to set things right, and a great deal of time will have been lost.

And when a translation is sold to an American publisher, the translator has every right to make clear and explain the reasons why certain words have been used, and how he or she approached the translation. In the hands of an inexperienced copyeditor, a novel can be heavily and blandly Americanized without consideration of the reasons behind the use of foreign words, names and terms. Sometimes an explanation is all that is required to ensure that key elements are retained in all editions.

TIMING

A critical point in contracts is timing. This will affect the UK publication, editions published in other English-speaking countries and maybe even more editions if English is being used as a source language from which other translations are made. There are often clauses in contracts with the original foreign publisher stating that the book must be published by a certain date. This can put commissioning editors in a difficult position, because they not only have to find a translator within this time frame, but they also have to have the book entirely translated, edited and marketed as well.

These pressures are often passed on to translators who may feel that they are given inadequate time to do the job properly. It's a difficult conundrum, with no obvious solution. On one hand, it is sensible for publishers to take advantage of the steam generated by a successful book in another language. For example, *Miss Smilla's Feeling for Snow*, by Peter Høeg, might not have done as well as it did in the UK if it had been published a year later. It fed on the excitement in Denmark, where it sat firmly on the bestseller lists. Similarly, *Suite Française* by Irène Némirovsky received outstanding reviews and international attention when it was published in France, and delaying an English edition too long would undoubtedly have squandered the benefits of this publicity.

Editors can find it difficult to motivate and inspire a sales team to market a book that has yet to be translated. No one can read it and get excited about it, often until the final months before publication, which can result in a serious loss of potential sales. One solution is for the translator to produce two or three chapters as quickly as possible, with a good synopsis and some translations of international reviews that the marketing department can use. It may be possible to breed enthusiasm by feeding the 'next instalment' through chapter by chapter, with great fanfare.

Most translators agree that it takes at least four to six months to make a good translation of a book of about 60,000 words. Ask translators how long they would like, and they might suggest anything from nine months to two years. The bottom line is that there is no point in rushing if it will jeopardise the translation. A poor translation is simply not worth publishing and will not only prevent decent sales but also dent faith in the publishing of foreign books in general. On the other hand translators must be aware that timing is important for the ultimate success of the book, and that what they perceive to be a 'rush' may well be necessary to achieve recognition and sales for the book.

PUBLICITY

In some cases, translators are asked to help publicise a book, particularly when an author speaks little or no English, or is unable or unwilling to travel. Although translators will obviously benefit financially from the increased sales that publicity will generate, it is not inappropriate to expect expenses to be paid, and a reasonable fee for the time spent on publicity. Similarly, translators should be paid for features written for newspapers or magazines to help publicise the book.

Once editors have chosen a translator for the job, they should start detailed discussions about how the translation should be approached, and what the communication channels should be. This not only makes the translator's job much easier, but also helps to ensure that the editor gets what he or she is expecting. There is no doubt that there are 'bad' translations, but these are not always the sole responsibility of the translator. Many are the result of crossed wires between editor and translator, or inadequate communication at the outset.

CONSULTATION WITH THE AUTHOR

As discussed on page 10 it can be very helpful for translators to have some access to the author in question, if possible, to answer queries and to explore issues or themes in the book that might require further explanation. Just because it has been edited and published in another language does not make a book perfect. There may be anomalies that need addressing, and even structural or other integral changes required. These will require the input and express permission of the author in most cases.

Translators need to know how and when they can contact the author, and within what parameters. If an author is being published simultaneously in several different languages, he or she might object to being subjected to an ongoing series of questions and discourse. It should be established at the outset what is acceptable. Most authors will be delighted by the interest and enthusiasm being shown for their book, and will relish the opportunity to discuss its fine details.

Robert Chandler, who translated *The Railway*, confesses to sending four or five hundred questions to author Hamid Ismailov in a single year, and, as he says, 'spending a lot of time together, discussing everything from obscene jokes to political slogans and Sufi literature.' Hamid welcomed this process. In an interview with Robert, he told him:

'I spent many years of my life translating classic and modern literature from one language to another: Russian to Uzbek, Uzbek to Russian, French to Uzbek, Uzbek to French, Turkish to Russian, English to Uzbek, etc., but I have never scrutinized any text so carefully as you scrutinized mine. Every single word was held up to the light. A writer is sometimes driven by some very personal association, or by the need for assonance or alliteration. As a result, he leaves some obscure places in his work. You exposed these. But you also helped to make me aware of deeper things.'

Robert believes that his relationship with Hamid was essential to the success of the translation. He says:

'There were scenes I did not understand because I did not know enough about Muslim life, scenes I did not understand because I did not know enough about Soviet life, and scenes where I was confused by the complexity of the interface between the two.

'Towards the end of my work on the novel I began to feel as if I were restoring a precious carpet. Patterns I had sensed only vaguely, as if looking at the underside of the carpet, began to stand out clearly; seemingly unimportant details in one chapter, I realized, reappeared as central themes of other chapters. Colours grew brighter as I sensed their inter-relationship. Occasionally I even felt able to suggest to Hamid that a particular thread should be moved from one part of the carpet to another.'

Shaun Whiteside, the translator of *Venice Is a Fish* by Tiziano Scarpa, is adamant about the importance of communication between translator and author, and believes that they should stay in touch even if there is a language divide. In some cases, a perfectly fluent translator will find it difficult to understand the prose and even the speech of some authors, but some contact, no matter how rudimentary, can still be invaluable. Shaun says:

'In the past I've tried to avoid troubling authors unless it was absolutely necessary, on the grounds that they probably had more pressing things to be getting on with. Now I reckon it's courteous at the very least to make contact from the beginning, as a relationship of trust is very important. With hindsight, I would have approached Tiziano at the start of the process rather than consulting him right at the end, and ideally met up with him rather than communicating only by e-mail.'

So what can you do if the author is deceased? To whom do you address questions, and how do you sort out points of confusion? In many cases family members, diaries, friends or scholarly journals can provide insight into vocabulary or inspiration. In others, there is simply no option but to guess, and hope that the resulting work is accurate. Like many translators who have to represent a time, culture or story that is past, Sandra Smith, who translated *Suite Française*, admits to being quite wary and nervous of the process. She was, however, happy to find that her concerns were groundless. She says:

'There were very few times when I had the feeling I was working from a draft. There was the odd sentence that didn't seem to make sense and when I asked several French friends, they also found that on close analysis there was some vagueness. These were very few and far between, however, and easily resolved, perhaps because Denise Epstein transcribed the novel from her mother's work journal and clearly did a very thorough job of deciphering. When you look at the original journal (now at the IMEC in Caen), you see that there are many crossings out, so Némirovsky did do some editing as she went along.'

Note: The Institut Mémoires de l'Edition Contemporaine, known in English as the Institute of Contemporary Publishing Archives, is a place where authors' original manuscripts are stored. The British Library in London has many original manuscripts, as do university departments worldwide. Family members should be able to indicate where originals are located.

CAPTURING THE STYLE

At an early meeting, the translator should ask the acquiring editor how the publishers are planning to market the book. If the twists and turns of a novel are being marketed as a slick whodunit, there may be language or certain elements of the book that need to be downplayed.

An experienced editor might have very clear ideas about how best to capture the author's style. He or she may have other books with a similar style that could indicate how the translation should be approached. There may also be other translations of the same author's work that strike the right chord, or can be used for comparative purposes—showing what the editor would and would not like to see.

If a sample of two or three thousand words is edited 'into style' by the editor, translators should not be dispirited or disillusioned by this exercise, as it will shed invaluable light on the editor's expectations. It is helpful to talk through the edit, line by line, to establish why an editor made changes, and how he or she thinks it improves the translation, as this will save time at later stages.

The book may end up being copyedited by a freelance editor or someone else in-house but this 'sample edit' can be used as a template for the remainder of the book. It also forms a sort of contract between editor and translator, who will have agreed on the style of the book on this basis.

TRANSLATION CHALLENGES

Areas that could present some difficulty in translation and, indeed, in the editing process, could include extensive use of dialect, humour, poetry or literary conceits, all of which will need to be approached in a systematic and pre-agreed manner. Will another translator or native speaker be called in to help get the dialogue right? Will humour be translated into English equivalents? Will poetry be translated at the same time, or will the translator look for existing English translations? Is it possible to keep up the same conceits? For example, if an author has managed to produce an entire book without using the equivalent of the word 'the,' is it conceivable that the same could be achieved in English?

All such issues that affect the book as a whole should be discussed with the editor before work commences, and an approach to the problems agreed. See Chapter Four for further discussion and some suggested solutions.

RESEARCH

Will research be required to clarify parts of the story? Most translators are accustomed to doing a great deal of research, normally before they begin to write, and this extra work should not only be built into the fee, but also the schedule. Quotations from other sources need to be tracked down in the English language in most cases. Translators customarily use online journals and other internet sources, and also become familiar with small collections of unusual works where they might be more likely to find obscure translations.

In some cases, travelling to the host country may be necessary. While translating *Venice Is a Fish* Shaun Whiteside soon realised that a trip to Venice would be essential in order to do the book justice. He says:

'Scarpa is one of the few writers of his generation to have grown up in Venice, and he brings to that city a freshness of vision that lingers in the mind. While advising visitors to walk around Venice "at random," he gently guides them in unexpected directions, pointing them towards the often bizarre details that might otherwise have escaped them—the anti-urine devices on the corners of buildings, for example, designed to splash the shoes and trousers of anyone foolish enough to want to relieve themselves in public. I had to check out little details—the nature and arrangement of the paving-stones, the railings along some of the canals, the anti-urine devices, the beautiful *forcole*—the carved gondola rowlocks—even visiting the backstreet workshop of a boatwright who makes them. And obviously it was important to try a *spriz*, the Venetian aperitif of white wine and Campari or a similar bitter. Tiziano advises against having more than one. I'm afraid I can confirm that his advice is very sensible.'

Even seasoned travellers and translators who are very familiar with the country in which a book is set may benefit from a repeat visit. Shaun Whiteside concluded that his second visit was invaluable, as he was able to see the book's setting through new eyes. He says:

'I had been there before, although with artist friends who introduced me to Tiepolo, and Veronese and (most importantly) Tintoretto. Tiziano Scarpa takes it as read that you will probably be able to find these masters for yourself, and guides you instead towards the unconsidered features of the city, hidden away in the back-streets or sitting unremarked at the top of a colonnade in St Mark's Square (the heart-rending story of the death of a child, told in comic-strip style). Consequently there's a free-wheeling freshness to his writing, a seemingly spontaneous mixture of the colloquial and the high-flown.'

TRANSLATORS AS EDITORS: A HANDS-ON APPROACH

Translators are also acting as editors during the process of translation. As they work word by word and line by line, anomalies and inconsistencies in the original will become clear, and structural problems that may have been missed by the original editor will emerge. There should, therefore, be a regular discourse between editor and translator throughout the process, to work out solutions to problems as they appear, rather than delivering a completed translation and finding out later on that something isn't acceptable. The author should be involved in the resolution of any major issues.

One way of managing this is for translators to keep notes about decisions made as they go along and include a list of notes to the editor when they deliver their translation, especially if the book is in a language the editor doesn't know. If the original has stylistic quirks, it's useful to mention these and point out that some of the choices are governed by them: for example, particularly long sentences, unusual punctuation or lack of it, repetition, use of dialect and slang, the inclusion of lots of 'foreign' words.

If translators choose to keep 'foreign' words, it can be useful to add a glossary at the end of the work, but this is a decision that needs to be made in consultation with the publisher and editor at the very beginning. For more information on using a glossary, see page 51.

TRANSLATORS' OTHER ROLES

Euan Cameron, former editor at Harvill and himself a translator, believes that the translator should be more widely involved in the publishing process. During the translation, he or she will be closest to the book and will probably know it better than anyone else apart from the author. Therefore, Euan suggests that translators check (and even help in the writing of) blurbs and sales material, as well as catalogue copy, and help to choose representative passages from the book to tempt the sales team and bookshops. If this hasn't already been done, translators can help to produce a file of translated press clippings from other countries. Once again, these extra roles should be built into the cost.

SCHEDULES

Most translators are aghast by the increasingly short schedules produced by publishers, and many editors will heartily agree. Not only are translators expected to produce a near-perfect work in just a few months, but time for editing is often not factored in. Rebecca Carter explains that schedules are not designed to inconvenience or confound people, but to get a book out 'in time.' UK sales teams ideally need material a year in advance of publication in order to plan an effective marketing campaign.

Rebecca has published a great many books in translation, and has found that there is sometimes confusion about timescales. One problem is that every country does things differently. Chinese authors, for example, are used to seeing their books in print just a month or two after submission and can't understand why it may take a year or more in the UK.

Whatever the schedule, translators must know in advance what is expected of them and when, and be made aware of any changes *en route*. If the schedule looks too tight for a reasonable translation, a solid editing stage and adequate time to read the proofs, translators must make their concerns clear at the outset, so that adjustments can be made. Ideally editors would also oppose extremely tight schedules, except when there are compelling reasons for a quick publication.

Being edited

In many cases the acquiring editor is not the person who will be working on the book on a line-by-line basis. Some editors deal only with structural changes, and work on getting the style and 'flavour' of the book right, while the nitty-gritty details are handed over to in-house or freelance copyeditors. In all cases, it's good practice for the translator to be aware of who is editing their book, and preferably in advance.

If a sample has been edited at the outset, both translator and editor know what to expect, and are working to the same guidelines. This should be shown to the copyeditor when he or she starts work, and a procedure should be established whereby the copyeditor can address queries to the translator, and they can both decide which queries need to be passed back to the author. We'll look at the editing process in more detail in Chapter Five. Ros Schwartz says:

'Translators need to stress their availability and willingness to work on the translation after they have delivered it. I sometimes have the feeling that publishers are surprised when we do this. I don't want to generalise, but it seems that publishers feel loath to go back to the translator if they feel the translation is unsatisfactory. They prefer to avoid a confrontation and ask someone else to "rescue" it. Then they swear they'll never touch another translation, it's all too complicated. But taking the time to give the translator feedback, giving him/her the chance to revise their work if it is unsatisfactory, is to invest in a long-term relationship. How else are translators to improve, working in isolation as they do? Investing a little time can reap long-term rewards in building trust and a solid working relationship.

'In an ideal world, a translation is the result of a constructive collaboration between publisher, translator, editor and sometimes the author too. Translation is a solitary profession and translators can be prickly about criticism. We need to be receptive to feedback and recognise that a translation can always be improved, and often a second pair of eyes is invaluable.'

Some translators have editors with whom they have worked particularly successfully in the past, and whom they would like to involve. Unless timing or costs don't work, it is definitely worth requesting your editor of choice and this may streamline the process considerably.

Most translators do not want to be simply handed a set of proofs without having had any communication with the copyeditor. Where changes are necessary, translators like to be given the opportunity to address them, rather than have the decisions imposed by someone else. There should be a discussion before editing starts about how proposed changes will be shown to the translator—whether marked up on paper, or tracked in a Word file.

STYLE SHEETS

It is always worth giving a house style sheet to the translator. If the book is being published in another English-speaking country, the translator should also be given a copy of the style sheet for the relevant publisher. Many translators wish to make changes for different markets themselves, which should always be encouraged as it will save time in the long run.

Every book is different and presents its own problems. Translators of literary fiction should be given scope to make critical decisions, in conjunction with the author and the editor, in order to produce the best possible book.

Martin Riker believes that making a book that evokes the spirit and particular energy of the original has to take precedence over making a book faithful to the original. He says that translators sometimes worry that steering away from a literal word-for-word translation will 'corrupt' the original text but says the fact is that a work in translation has already been corrupted by the act of translation itself. The new work, the translated work, is already an interpretation of the original, and unavoidably so.

So the question should rather be: what sort of interpretation conveys the experience of the original, its particular stylistic energy, most accurately? The translation should not preserve literal words and phrases for preservation's sake. To treat a translated book in this way is to treat it more as a museum piece than as a vibrant literary work, says Martin. He urges translators to use their own creative writing skills to adapt the original, and cites this example:

'The British translator Barbara Wright has time and again taken great liberties in her translations of the French poet and novelist

Raymond Queneau. If she did not take such liberties, if she did not see herself as an artist who takes artistic risks, readers of her translations would have no way to access the playful brilliance of Queneau. Translated word for word, Queneau would fall flat.'

TITLES

Literal translations of titles will often fail to grab the prospective audience for the book. Sometimes a complete change is required to make the book saleable in English-speaking countries, and difficult decisions may have to be made. Ultimately, the title is a commercial decision on which the publisher will have the final say, but creating a bland new title in order to avoid alienating readers is not good practice. The editor (with ammunition from the translator and possibly the author) should stand his or her ground, and offer more viable solutions that better reflect the book.

Sandra Smith, who translated *Suite Française*, was concerned about the decision to leave the title in French—particularly for the American market. She worried that readers would assume they had to go into a specialist French bookshop to order it, but was proved wrong on all counts. *Suite Française* was one of the top 100 bestselling books in the UK in 2007, and did equally well in America.

Primo Levi was often vocally outraged by changes made to the titles of his books. For example, the title of *If This Is a Man* is an integral part of the book, but it was changed in the American edition to *Escape from Auschwitz*—a label he considered inept and vulgar. His title *Meccano d'amore* was naively translated as the hardly compelling *Love's Erector Set*. *La chiave a stella* was published in the US as *The Monkey's Wrench*. The Italian title specifically means a socket wrench, and adding the apostrophe compounds the error.

So literal translations are often a dreadful mistake when it comes to titles, and editors and translators must be prepared to be creative. Some titles lend themselves neatly to English translations; for example, *La sombra del viento* was the original Spanish title for the international bestseller *The Shadow of the Wind*, by Carlos Ruiz Zafón. But others do not, and a misleading and off-putting title can badly damage potential sales.

Stylised language

Translating a book written in a particular style (baroque, for example), even when written by contemporary authors, poses its own problems. Do translators 'update' the text to refresh it and make it accessible, thereby losing distinctive use of vocabulary and turn of phrase, or do they labour to match it? No one would expect to read Shakespeare in modern English (apart, perhaps, from lazy students), nor would they expect to lose the beauty of Francesc Fontanella's or Francesc Vicenç Garcia's prose by having it written in a contemporary style.

If the author is alive, his or her help will be invaluable. Robert Chandler says that he could not have unravelled the sometimes-baroque syntax and deftly interwoven stories of *The Railway* without author Hamid's help. But translators may not always have this option, and artistic licence is required. In older works, translators are often required to source and examine original material and critiques in both languages in order to establish the correct mood, tone and style.

Another stylistic problem can be presented by purposeful awkwardness in the original that simply does not work in the new language. There's always a danger that it will just read like a bad translation. You can try to convey the sense of awkwardness in other ways—by subtly referring to it, for instance, or moving direct dialogue into indirect, etc.—but sometimes you simply have to leave the passage out. Something will have been lost, but the important thing is that the translation should not call attention to itself in a way that will mar the reader's experience of the book.

REGIONAL DIALECTS

There's a fine line between making foreign authors accessible to English-speaking readers and making them sound like English writers. The rhythms and patterns of their own languages are part of what makes them interesting and it can be a mistake to iron them out completely.

Hanan al Shaykh, the Lebanese author of *The Sands of Zahra* and *Women of Sand and Myrrh*, is no stranger to the complexities of the process of translating and has often argued for dialect phrases to be kept in her books. In one example, she had a character say: 'My heart was pounding as if it was wearing wooden clogs.' This is the direct translation of a phrase in a southern dialect of Arabic, and Hanan wanted to keep it but her translator said it sounded clunky in English. Hanan, however, stuck to her guns and it stayed in. After that she started getting more involved in her translations because she wants to maintain the idioms of the original language in her work.

Sometimes the idiom needs a little explanation for English readers. In another example, she wrote: 'I thought she must be imagining that a hyena had pissed on our leg.' In Arabic, this phrase means 'to hypnotise and capture.' In English, the translator had to add, 'I thought she must be imagining that a hyena had pissed on our leg and stolen us away to its lair.' It didn't make sense without this addition.

Hanan says, 'Many people think of Arabic as an archaic, classical, old language, as in the Qu'ran, but you need to approach it with a modern outlook. You can't be entirely faithful—sometimes you need to explain it as well.'

While leaving in too many 'unknown' cultural references will weaken a book, and lose readers, there must, still, be an essence of something different. Some languages need lengthy explanations, which can be cumbersome, and force the translator to rely on glossaries and notes in order to provide the necessary explanations.

STRONG LANGUAGE

Expletives that are integral to a book should always remain. The difficulty lies in making the language accessible and relevant, without offending more delicate sensibilities. In some cultures, swearing is an everyday activity, whereas in many English-speaking countries bad language is considered to be less acceptable and gratuitous swearing may be frowned upon. Another problem, too, is the wealth of expletives in other languages, which simply cannot be matched by English equivalents.

Martin Riker notes that often a translator will 'clean up' the strong language in the original without even realizing, simply because he or she is not comfortable with it, even though the original writer was. This happens more often than one would expect, and translators tend to realize it only after an editor has pointed it out.

Robert Chandler encountered problems with foul language when translating *The Railway*. He says:

'Curses and swearwords present a particular problem for translators into contemporary English. Our lexicon of abusive language is oddly limited, and the more florid curses still common in Russian tend to sound laughable if translated at all literally. Reluctantly, I simplified much of the foul language. In one chapter I tried to compensate for this impoverishment by adding my own brief evocation of the essence of Russian mat or foul language: "those monstrous, magnificent, multi-layered and multi-storied variations on pricks and cunts and mother-fucking curs."'

COLLOQUIALISMS

Similar considerations apply to colloquialisms as to expletives. Martin Riker says that the most important issue with slang is timeliness—will the approximate slang chosen by the translator remain relatively current? With some translations you can almost identify the year, if not the month, in which it must have been translated, especially when it comes to teenage slang.

Once again, it can be a question of getting exactly the right translator for the job. Euan Cameron says that with Argentine writers such as Edgardo Cozarinsky or Alan Pauls, he looked for a translator who was sensitive to the cultural and colloquial differences in Argentine Spanish, and found the ideal person in Nick Caistor, who had lived in Argentina for many years. It can also help to employ a second translator, with a good working knowledge of colloquialisms, dialect and slang in the native country, who can get across their meaning and help to come up with English equivalents that are appropriate, do not jar with the reader and, most importantly, do not date.

HUMOUR

Just as slang or colloquialisms often fail to translate, so humour can present a problem for translators. Something hugely funny in another language can fall flat in English, without lengthy explanations that certainly reduce any humour involved. Equivalents may simply be out of context with the book itself, and often seem nonsensical. Robert Chandler says:

'Humour, of course, tends to be what gets lost most easily in translation. We speak of jokes being "barbed" or "pointed," and jokes do indeed have something in common with darts or arrows. If a

47

joke is to survive the journey into another language, if it is to hit the mark even when its cultural context can no longer be taken for granted, its point may need to be adjusted or somehow re-sharpened. A sentence about "Bolta-Lightning" [the English nickname chosen for the town electrician in *The Railway*] sounded irritatingly plodding even after several revisions. It was only after my wife suggested replacing the literal "explained to" by the wittier "explained over the heads of" that the English version began to seem as funny as the original: "Bolta-Lightning climbed the column in the middle of the square, hung the banner on the loudspeaker and explained over the heads of the entire backward bazaar both the progressive meaning of the slogan and the precise time the proletariat was to unite."'

He goes on to say:

'There is often an element of paradox in the work of a translator; I have never before had to work so hard to understand the literal meaning of the original text—and I have never before allowed myself to depart from the literal meaning so often and so freely. Not every pun in the original is translatable, and I have omitted jokes that needed too much explanation; I have compensated, I hope, by gratefully accepting any appropriate pun that English offered. Sometimes these puns seemed to arise without any effort on my part; it would have been hard, for example, for an English translator to avoid a pun (a pun not present in the original) in the passage where the sight of Nasim's huge "male member" makes Khaira "remember" facts about her life that she had forgotten for decades.'

Martin Riker agrees that the most successful translations of jokes are more likely to be replacements than literal translations—replacing jokes from the original language with a comparable joke in the new one. He thinks that humour translates more often than 'jokes,' *per se*.

Plays on words are obviously specific to their original language. An equivalent has to be found in the new language and sometimes these simply don't work or need to be cut, or a completely different play on words has to be invented to retain the liveliness of play. In such cases, the translator and editor might have to decide which is more important to the passage—the literal sense of the phrase or the playfulness that it brings to bear.

A fresh pair of eyes can be particularly helpful when it comes to translating humour. It is no coincidence that many comedians write in couples or even teams.

UNTRANSLATABLE WORDS AND CULTURE-SPECIFIC REFERENCES

When translating Tiziano Scarpa's *Venice Is a Fish* Shaun Whiteside had to rely on extensive discussions with the author as well as a great deal of research to work out English equivalents for some of the more specialist vocabulary. He says:

'The incredibly helpful author, who speaks impeccable English, was very keen to help with the list of fish—*sea bass, gilthead, dentice, umbrine*, etc. Tiziano was also very solicitous about the more arcane snack-foods—*marsioni* (goby), *schie* (shrimp), *nervetti* (pork or beef tendon). That was incredibly helpful, as these dishes tend to be local to the city.'

Martin Riker says:

'If references are not obscure or difficult for the original audience, they should not be obscure or difficult for the new audience. Of course there are real limits to the extent to which it is possible to make such references familiar, but certain simple tricks can contextualize for the reader without damaging their experience of the book. For example, you can add an inconspicuous explanatory phrase, or mention that So-and-so is a "town," or add the word "Avenue" where it was left out of the original. Here as elsewhere the translation editor has to assume the position of the reader, and should consider the overall experience of reading the original and how best to approximate that experience for readers in English.'

If readers will baulk at *croque monsieur*, it's easy to add an unobtrusive description (for example, 'the cheese oozed over the salty ham of his *croque monsieur* sandwich') to enlighten them. There is no reason, either, why general explanations cannot be offered from time to time; for example, adding 'three miles out of the city' after a town that someone local to the region would know instinctively, adding a paragraph describing the ingredients of a particularly native culinary dish, or even giving background to a cultural practice or event by giving a character more dialogue. Sometimes it's best to be vague, e.g., substituting 'a fragrant spice mix' for *Ras al-hanut* (Moroccan).

Some words, however, simply don't translate. Ros Schwartz usually prefers to leave these in the text and to provide the reader with a glossary, which can serve the purpose of explaining more obscure geographical and cultural references, without interrupting the flow of the text with lengthy descriptions and explanations. A map can also prove invaluable for readers. Eliminating traces of foreignness completely can iron out the quirks and flatten the text, and this is a potential problem that calls for vigilance.

Euan Cameron feels that it is expecting a lot for translators to get beneath the surface of the words and convey cultural anomalies without relying upon footnotes to some extent. He says:

'At Harvill we published several novels by Pierre Magnan, a writer who lives and sets all his work in Provence, and uses many Provençal words and expressions. Patricia Clancy, his translator, had particular problems to resolve how to deal with these and to convey the right tone without using too many footnotes.'

She was successful in coming up with solutions, but in the end footnotes may be the only option, and they are certainly a better alternative to lengthy discourses interrupting the flow of the text.

QUOTATIONS FROM OTHER SOURCES

In most cases, it is good practice to seek out existing English translations of quotes or material such as poetry or song lyrics, rather than re-translating—not only because of the time constraints involved in creating associations and rhythm between the words of yet *another* author, but because it is, in essence, a different 'art.' The demands of finding equivalent vocabulary that is as rich with allusions and meaning, along with recreating rhythm and rhyme can pose an insurmountable problem. It is, however, often necessary for a translator to do the work him or herself, because there is no English equivalent available. Robert Chandler says:

'Sometimes I spend days looking for a synonym for a particular word or trying to improve the rhythm of a particular line of poetry. And then, after wasting a lot of time, I realize that the problem is not in the place where I thought it was. If I change something in the previous verse or sentence, then the problem disappears just like that.'

Some quotes simply do not translate, and are best dropped. Others must be altered to make their meaning and relevance to the text clear. In these cases, a translator must be given some licence to make appropriate changes—dropping the original rhyme structure, for example, or altering the rhythm. A direct replacement might also be necessary, in the case of lyrics, for example, to something that has the right resonance with English readers. These are all choices that must be made *en route* to the final translation, and which should be discussed with the author and the editor. In many cases, the author may be able to provide insight into something that completely befuddles both editor and translator. Sometimes a footnote explaining the meaning of the poem or quote, and leaving it in its original language, is the best alternative.

A note should be made of any other sources from which translations are taken and given to the copyeditor along with the translator's notes. In some cases, permission may be required to reproduce someone else's translation.

'DIFFICULT' LANGUAGES

There are some languages for which high-quality translators are few and far between, forcing publishers either to abandon the idea of translating, or to rely on the joint efforts of a prose stylist and a native-speaker to get the balance right. It may also be necessary to translate from a separate language altogether, because a good native translator simply can't be found.

English is often the key bridging language into other languages—a translator in India will be more likely to be able to translate a book from English than from Finnish or Dutch, for example. Thus, to publish an excellent translation in English is to open up possibilities of further translation of that title into other languages throughout the world. This should be a point of pride for translators, for their role will be much greater than simply introducing an author and recreating his or her book for a new audience, and it's something that should be borne in mind throughout the writing process. What would *other* cultures make of what you are writing?

A translator whose work will be re-used in this way should be paid a fee for that re-use, and given a proper acknowledgement or credit in the new translation. Also, permission would need to be cleared with the rights holders of both the English-language translation and the original work.

Historically, the lack of good translators working in a specific language may have deterred readers from picking up literature in translation. Hanan al Shaykh tells how, as a child, she was confused by an Arabic translation of Stefan Sweig's *Troubled Souls*, in which a cat appeared to go to the fridge for a glass of milk, changing his mind and deciding in favour of a whisky instead. How can a cat do all this, she wondered? She asked her teacher at school, who had a German husband, and he worked out that the Arabic translator had translated the German *Herr* ('mister') as the similar-sounding Arabic word for cat. This was her first experience of the effects of bad translation and put her off reading literature in translation for a long time. But she says that now they have some brilliant translators working into Arabic and the whole area has opened up.

A TRANSATLANTIC COMPROMISE

If the translator is aware that the book will be published in the US as well as the UK, it's a good idea to look for compromises at the outset. Providing a transatlantic text may be preferable to having to Americanize it later, which is more work and likely to be unpaid.

It is in no one's interests for the work to be 'dumbed down' for either market, and therefore finding words that work as well in either country will prevent inappropriate substitutions being made at a later date. Sometimes it's best to avoid problematic words and find a suitable description instead. For example, a 'chocolate nut bar' will work better than a 'Yorkie' or a 'Reese's.'

Sandra Smith was aware of the potential pitfalls of transatlantic publishing at the outset. She says:

'When I was translating *Suite Française* I was aware that it was going to be published both in the UK and America. Wherever there was an instance of a very British phrase that I thought Americans wouldn't understand I would put a slash and put the American phrase next to it but when it came to be published they ignored them all and just published the UK version, which surprised me. The exception was "gherkins," which are, of course, "pickles" in the US. They even left the phrase "She's canny," which surprised me because I wasn't sure that Americans would understand what canny means.'

Translators will, ideally, discuss with the UK and US editor at the outset whether transatlantic style is required and how far it should go.

A HEALTHY BALANCE

Anglicising a book too heavily detracts from the power of the book, and its unique qualities. It simply tells a story in a palatable way, rather than creating an impression of the culture in which it is set. A good translation allows a reader to experience first hand a different world—hearing the sounds, tasting local fare, seeing the sights and what lies beneath them, and feeling what the protagonists feel, and what the author wants them to feel. Robbing a book of its significant differences does it an injustice, and this should be avoided at all cost. Sometimes translators have to fight long and hard to retain these differences, but it is a battle worth fighting.

Robert Chandler succinctly describes the decision processes he went through:

'*The Railway* reminds me in some ways of a jazz improvisation or the paintings of Paul Klee. Hamid keeps to a delicate balance between imposing order on words and staying open to suggestions from words, between telling a clear story and allowing words to dance their own dance. In translating the novel, I have tried to observe a similar balance—both to be attentive to precise shades of meaning and to listen out for unexpected ways in which English might be able to reproduce the music of the original. Fidelity, after all, is never simply a mechanical matter. To stay faithful to people or things you love, there are times when you need to draw on all your resources of creativity and imagination. If I appear to have taken liberties with the original, it has been in the hope of being faithful to it at a deeper level.

'I have never—I hope—simplified anything of cultural importance. The character known as Mullah-Ulmas-Greeneyes, for example, is not really a mullah; "Mullah" is a nickname, given to him by people around him because it alliterates with "Ulmas." One reader suggested I omit this "Mullah," arguing that English readers are not used to Muslims using religious terms so light-heartedly and would find the word confusing. This had the effect of bringing home to me how important it was to keep the "Mullah." The Muslim world has never been monolithic; Central Asia has nearly always been religiously liberal—with Sufis having the upper hand over dogmatists—and during the Soviet period secularism made considerable inroads. Even believers tended not to take their religion over-seriously.'

SUMMING UP THE TRANSLATOR'S ROLE

A good translator will:
- Bring creative energy and imagination to the work, without losing the author's style, message or unique flavour.
- Think carefully about substitutions or changes, and discuss major changes with the acquiring editor.
- Take heed of an editor's fresh approach to the text, and remember that he or she will be seeing it with new eyes, and judging it as English prose.
- Strike a fine balance between making the book accessible to new readers, while still maintaining its essential 'foreignness' and differences.
- Remember that not all books are perfect, and that even tiny tweaks (made in conjunction with an editor) can make a good book brilliant.
- Keep careful notes of changes and decisions made in the process of translating.
- Take careful consideration of humour, puns, jokes and literary allusions, names of places and characters, as well as cultural references and ideology.

- Correctly translate idiomatic expressions, which lend colour and flavour.
- Consider and represent the author's culture, without turning it into a cultural treatise.
- Carefully recreate the nuances of the original language.

Translators will not:
- Take major liberties with the author's text without reference to both editor and author.
- Anglicise a book beyond recognition.
- Play with the structure or the sequence of time or events, except in consultation with the author or editor.
- Refuse help from the author, editor or another translator; every insight, every set of eyes, provides a new depth of understanding, and possible resolutions to difficulties faced.

Having established a good relationship with the acquiring editor, a translator can be dumbfounded to find that the editorial work on the book will be undertaken by someone else. It is, however, common practice for acquiring editors to get the job started and then hand it over to someone who will work directly on the text. In some cases, the original editor will do the structural editing (looking at the overall approach, taking into consideration the foundation and infrastructure of the book, including its style, tempo, overall use of language, characterisation and sequence of events), and pass the line-by-line work to a copyeditor, who will address individual words and sentences, punctuation and grammar, and points of inconsistency or inaccuracy. In other instances, all editorial work will be done by one editor, who may be in-house or freelance.

THE ROLE OF THE STRUCTURAL EDITOR

An editor should look at the overall book, not the 'translation,' and edit it as an original book. In some cases, editors are reluctant to make changes to a translation, on the basis that it has already been 'edited' and published in another language. But different publishing houses in other countries have different editorial standards. In Euan Cameron's experience, 'European editors make very few alterations to an author's text, and tend to regard the author's word as sacrosanct. British editors, I think, are more intrusive, and Americans even more so.' In his opinion, a good editor should not consider the job complete until the book is as perfect as it can be, no matter how successful or good the original.

Martin Riker says:

'The act of translation often seems to "canonize" a book as it appeared in its original language. The types of editorial decisions that are made every day for works written in English—to rework a weak piece of dialogue, for example—become unthinkable with translations, simply by virtue of the fact that the book, having already been published in one language, is perceived as being "done." This is particularly problematic when, as often happens, the book was not edited well in its original language, and will contain obvious logistical problems: someone walks out of a room and then, in the next scene, is still standing in it—or of course any number of less obvious problems that nonetheless work against the book's succeeding at what it is trying to do.

'We should think of the editor of a translated work as playing two editorial roles: editor of the translation and editor of the book. There is no reason why a book should not be edited simply because it has already appeared in another form (language), if the original form is flawed, and assuming that the editor is proceeding responsibly. My experience is that foreign writers are most often thankful that problems in their work are being caught and addressed, and are happy to work with us on improvements.'

Euan Cameron has met resistance though:

'On the few occasions I have ever asked foreign authors to make cuts or consider revising passages of their text prior to acquiring rights, I've met with a blunt refusal. This is understandable—"If it's OK in my own language," they say, "why change?"'

If the translator has been well chosen and the major translation decisions have been discussed along the way, wide-scale changes should not be needed at the editing stage. Many translators are instinctive editors and, because they are so close to the text and often agonise over single words and sentences for hours or even days, they are in a position to spot anomalies and address them long before the editor has clapped eyes on them. Most translators go through the text several times and, in the end, know it as intimately as the author.

Euan feels that it is important to assume that a translator is an authority on the language in question, and that editing a translation is more to do with style, usage, pace, tone and colloquialisms, which are, he thinks, more of a copyeditor's role. Structural editing should be largely unnecessary.

So unless the acquiring editor is going to be doing the line-by-line copyediting work, his or her main responsibilities are to find an appropriate translator, create and maintain a good working relationship with him or her, liaise with the author about suggested changes and progress, reassure the author of the merits of the translator, and finally to stand up for the book within the publishing house.

A good copyeditor adjusts and tinkers unobtrusively to create the book that both author and translator envisaged. A good copyedit appears effortless and changes are normally such that they are not even recognised. Yet a copyeditor brings a fresh pair of eyes and will spot anomalies that translators may have missed on even a third or fourth reading.

According to Christina Thomas, from The Society for Editors and Proofreaders, a copyeditor has several aims. These include producing a book that:

- Is free from typographical and grammatical errors, and well punctuated.
- Conforms to the publisher's house style, with consistencies of spelling and usage.
- Is consistent on every level: facts are consistent (if the heroine's eyes are blue on page 5 they must still be blue on page 79; a gin-drinker won't suddenly have a glass of bourbon in his hand); the arguments hold together; and internal inconsistencies should be spotted and rectified.
- Is factually accurate. While the author and the translator are responsible for factual research, the copyeditor should be able to spot and query things that 'jar' or do not make sense. If references are unclear to the copyeditor, the chances are they will be to the reading public, too. The copyeditor should query such instances with the translator and ask him or her to clarify.
- Is written in graceful, flowing and elegant English that is appropriate to its subject matter and amongst other things free

of redundant words, overuse of clichés and awkward formulations. Perhaps the most difficult part of the copyeditor's job to define is style. Redundant, superfluous and unnecessary words, phrases and sentences that are used when they are not needed are simple enough to spot; clichés can be eliminated or toned down, and a copyeditor will have to use common sense to spot when a translator has, perhaps, settled on a misleading or unhelpful analogy or metaphor. Repetitious vocabulary must be tackled. In English we don't like using the same word too often; we've got a wide vocabulary and we like to exercise it.

- Copyeditors have to look out for unacceptable or controversial usage. For example, Christina says, 'I gather from my Texan cousin that it's no longer acceptable to talk about blacks in Texas, whereas here in the UK it doesn't raise an eyebrow. More thorny issues might be references to Israel, Palestine and the Occupied Territories, or Kurdistan being referred to as a country.'

- A copyeditor should also be on the lookout for anything contentious that might fall foul of the libel laws.

- And they should be looking for any quoted matter that might require permission to reproduce. It's their job to flag these matters, not to resolve them.

Christina says that a copyeditor has to treat the voice of the translator as the voice of the author and try to make that voice consistent. She also confirms that a good copyeditor doesn't try to re-write a book in their own voice or over-correct language that may sound awkward for good reason (perhaps because it is technical or colloquial).

Books from so many countries are now published in English that it is highly unlikely any publishing house will have editors that are fluent in all the languages. The most important thing is that a book being published in English should be *edited* in English, because this is the language in which the book is being read. Martin Riker believes that the editor's primary concern must be towards the quality of the work in English, so that it creates for an English-language reader an experience approximate to the experience the book's original readers had. The editor first and foremost must be a reader of English, and a person for whom the translation must read, in English, like an original work—which in many senses it is.

Knowledge of the language in question can, however, be an advantage, particularly at the copyediting stage. Some people suggest that a copyeditor should read a translation line-by-line against the original book but this seems an extravagant and unnecessary effort. The copyeditor's job is to ensure that the book works in its own right, rather than as a faithful translation. However, when things don't seem to be working, it can be useful for an editor to check the original source text to see if there is an easy solution, or if an error has been made.

Ultimately, though, editors must trust a good translator, and assume that every effort has been made to translate accurately. Queries can be addressed to the translator, who will have made decisions about every word choice and can defend or explain their use. It's very likely that a translator will already have consulted the author about issues that are unclear, or areas where there is some confusion, and so he or she will be in a position to explain or justify.

WHAT MAKES A GOOD EDITOR?

Ros Schwartz feels that the most important quality is empathy. Just as the translator needs to empathize with the text, so does the editor. She also feels that a shared sensibility is vital for producing the best possible translation. Matching the editor to the book and the translator is as important as matching the translator to the book. Ros says:

'Every translator hopes that his or her editor will manage to put a finger on things that are odd or bumpy, but rather than start rewriting, indicate instead places where they feel something is wrong and offer the opportunity to revisit what I've done. Suggestions pencilled in the margin may or may not be the best solution, but often an editor's prodding will nudge a translator towards finding a better option. What is not helpful is when editors intervene randomly, merely substituting synonyms which do not improve the translation, or worse, introduce errors, or question words they can't be bothered to check in the dictionary.

'A good editor is like a midwife—he or she helps bring forth that perfectly formed translation that is inside you but doesn't necessarily emerge unaided.'

Across the board, translators request that editors should discuss corrections with them and give them the opportunity to rectify problems themselves. Asking 'Is this an improvement?' rather than making a change is a better way to deal with editing, particularly if a translator is sensitive.

Most translators prefer seeing proposed editorial changes on paper rather than on screen. Some even relish the opportunity to take in corrections themselves, allowing them to consider every change and the various alternatives, before they become final. Changes can be tracked in Word, though this can make the text difficult to read and assess. It's a good idea for editors to speak to translators early in the process, show a sample of how they intend to edit, and then find out how the translator would prefer to see the suggested changes. Ideally editors will take into consideration translators' views and opinions.

It is important that translators are given the opportunity (and an adequate amount of time) to read edited text and then the proofs, so that errors unwittingly introduced by the editor, or changes made that alter something important in the sense, flow or integrity of the book can be addressed. Translators are not only defending their own work when they challenge suggested changes, but the work of the author as well.

In the event of a dispute

Most translators have not worked in a publishing house, and are unaware of the pressures involved (progress meetings to report to, sales targets to be met, paper to be ordered, printing slots that can be lost if text is even a day late, and so forth). While maintaining the integrity of the book they are translating, it's possible that they will overlook the commercial importance of the project. If the acquiring editor involves the translator at every stage, and gives them a clear idea of the schedule and why it has been structured in the way it has, this can help to overcome difficulties.

Good communication is the key all round. If the publishing process is clearly explained to the translator, he or she will understand why late corrections can cause problems, why it creates difficulties if the translation is delivered a couple of weeks late, and so forth. Conflict with editors can be avoided if translators explain in advance what they intend to do. By establishing a good relationship at the outset, and taking time to maintain it, most problems can be ironed out easily.

Rarely will a translator and editor see eye to eye on every matter, and there has to be some give and take, some compromise on both parts. An editor should recognise that the translator is, for the moment, the expert party and, as long as the brief has been made clear, and agreed to by the translator, the editor should assume that the translation is correct and has been carefully undertaken. A translator is invested with the responsibility of making many decisions, and there must be a degree of trust involved to allow him or her to get on with the job.

Equally, however, translators must expect criticism and queries, as well as constructive suggestions for changes. Most translators speak fondly of the help they've received from very hands-on editors, and how they were able to address the more challenging parts of the text together. Sandra Smith even says that she felt her American publishers hadn't edited her enough and she went back and made more changes herself as a result.

Rebecca Carter says that her worst-case scenario would be a translator who couldn't see that her editorial suggestions were an improvement:

'The editorial process relies on trust, and that trust only develops when a translator thinks, "Ah, I see exactly why she has queried that word/sentence, and now I know how to put it right." If that doesn't happen, then everything can break down. I have experienced a situation where the translator thought I had completely misunderstood the text. Perhaps I had. The book was in Russian, not a language that I could read or whose literature I could claim to be an expert on. However, I had attempted to find a way to make the language flow in English. The translator believed that I was deliberately 'commercialising' the book. Translators, quite rightly, often feel themselves the defender of an author's original and can find themselves in a difficult situation if the editor takes issue with elements of the text that the translator thinks are completely faithful to the original. Hopefully discussion can bring about compromise, with the editor understanding better why the translator has made certain choices, and the translator coming to see why certain passages of their translation don't work for the reader. In the case I am talking about, I had made the fatal mistake of not leaving enough time for such discussions to take place.'

So who makes the final decision if there is a stalemate? The simple answer is the acquiring editor. He or she represents the author to some extent, should have the best interests of the translator at heart, and also has the experience necessary to make decisions that will protect the commercial interests of the book. It should ideally never reach the stage of impasse, but if it does, the editor must have the final word.

If the translator is very unhappy with changes made, he or she has the option of taking his or her name off the book altogether, but that is a last resort that no party involved would welcome.

CAN BAD TRANSLATIONS BE REWRITTEN?

What constitutes a bad translation? If a book has been translated accurately but lacks the magic that was integral to the original, then it may be possible to salvage the text by introducing a prose stylist or a very good English editor. In other words, a 'flat' translation may not necessarily be an unsalvageable translation.

If a translation has, however, lost not just its integral flow and the style of the author, but also its literal meaning, it can be harder to rescue. Engaging an external reader to assess the main areas where the book fails is a good first step, and it may be possible to rectify the problems with the involvement of a native speaker. The external reader's report should be shown to the translator and he or she should be given an opportunity to make amends, if possible. If, however, the translation has strayed too far from the original, it may need to be retranslated, and the costs absorbed.

In this instance, there may be contractual points that an editor can use to reclaim some of the translator's fee, particularly if there was a good editorial brief and some sample translated text attached to the contract. But the assessment of the final product is often subjective, and it may be difficult to get the translator to agree that the finished product is not acceptable. This is one reason why working closely with a translator throughout the process is worthwhile—potential problem areas will be flagged early on and a translator can be redirected as necessary, or an appropriate second person brought in to address the areas where assistance is needed.

Summing up the editor's role

A good editor will:
- Approach the text as an original book rather than a translation.
- Bring a fresh pair of eyes to the text, pinpointing any areas that do not work, making suggestions about solutions to problems and discussing them with the translator.
- Highlight inconsistencies, clichés, libel and repetition, and refer them back to the translator.
- Correct any errors of spelling, grammar and punctuation, and ensure the text conforms to the publisher's house style.
- Show their editorial corrections to the translator, either as pencil markings on paper, or tracked in Word, before it is too late to correct any errors that have crept in.
- Respect the voice of the translator and treat him or her as they would any original author.

Editors will not:

- Rewrite the text in their own voice, changing vocabulary choices that the translator has made.
- Over-Anglicise and sanitise the foreignness of the text.
- Make changes that will not be visible to the translator and then send the edited text for typesetting without showing it to the translator.

CHAPTER SIX: ONGOING RELATIONSHIPS

THE TRANSLATOR'S ROLE AFTER EDITING IS COMPLETE

To maintain the relationship, the editor should keep the translator informed about publicity plans, reviews that appear (both favourable and not), sales figures, subsequent rights sales and marketing initiatives. It is good practice to invite the translator to a book's launch party. Translators may also like to present the book at a sales conference, or give readings in local libraries and bookshops to help promote the book.

When problems arise after the translator has finished the job—perhaps in subsequent editions when changes are suggested to the translator's original copy, to make it appropriate for another market—the translator should be kept abreast of the situation. If commercial decisions are made that the translator is unhappy about, the editor should, ideally, act as a go-between, passing back concerns. At the very least the editor can represent their own views and those of the translator to the new publisher.

TRANSLATORS' NETWORKS

The network of good translators is still relatively small, but it is vibrant and important. We have already seen how successful a collaborative translation can be, and more and more translators are choosing to work together to create the best possible books. It's good practice to encourage networks, and everyone benefits. The Translators' Association, a subsidiary of the Society of Authors (www.societyofauthors.org) is a good place to start making new contacts, and the British Centre for Literary Translation also runs an online discussion board (www.literarytranslation.com).

In Conclusion . . .

Both translator and editor are seeking the same goal—a high-quality novel that does justice to the original text while being accessible and compelling for readers in the new market. We believe that following the 'best practice' guidelines outlined above will help to achieve this goal.

SELECTED DALKEY ARCHIVE PAPERBACKS

FOR A FULL LIST OF PUBLICATIONS, VISIT:
www.dalkeyarchive.com

SELECTED DALKEY ARCHIVE PAPERBACKS

FOR A FULL LIST OF PUBLICATIONS, VISIT:
www.dalkeyarchive.com